•DISCOVERING•
MARS
The Amazing Story of the Red Planet

by Melvin Berger

with illustrations by Joan Holub

SCHOLASTIC INC.
New York   Toronto   London   Auckland   Sydney

ISBN 0-590-45221-5

17 16 15 14 13 12 11 10 9   7 8 9/9 0 1 2/0

Printed in the U.S.A.   23

First Scholastic printing, October 1992

Revised edition, September 1997

Book design by Laurie Williams

For Benny

Birth of Mars

Pretend you can go far, far back in time to about five billion years ago. Huge clouds of dust and gas are swirling around in space. Each cloud stretches across trillions of miles.

As time goes by, the dust and gas pull closer together. The clouds shrink, but they are still huge. They are now millions of miles across.

Each of these clouds forms a star. One of these stars is our sun.

Now pretend it is a few million years later. Some leftover bits of dust and gas remain in space. They keep whirling about and bumping into each other all around the sun.

Some dust and gas stick together. They form bigger and bigger pieces. They take on the shape of a ball called a sphere. Each sphere becomes a planet. The planets keep on whirling around the sun. But they are much smaller than the sun.

There are nine planets: Mercury, Venus, Earth, Mars, Jupiter, Saturn, Uranus, Neptune, and Pluto.

Mars is the fourth planet from the sun. It is Earth's neighbor in space.

A Strange Planet

People have always seen three objects in the sky:

The sun — sending out its powerful heat and light.

The moon — changing shape throughout the month.

Mars — looking different from the other planets and stars.

What makes Mars different?

Mars is deep red in color!

This photograph of Mars was taken by a telescope on Earth. It does not show as many details as the photo on the front cover, which was taken from a spacecraft.

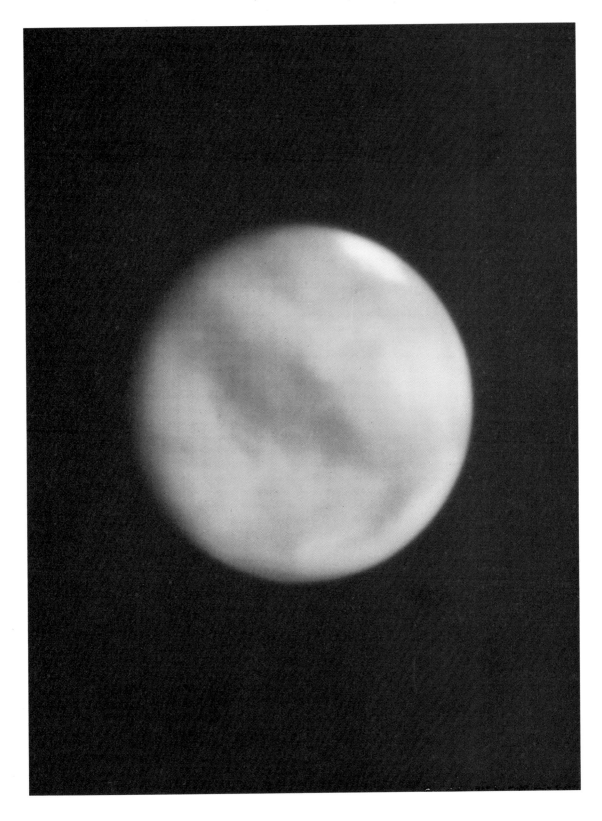

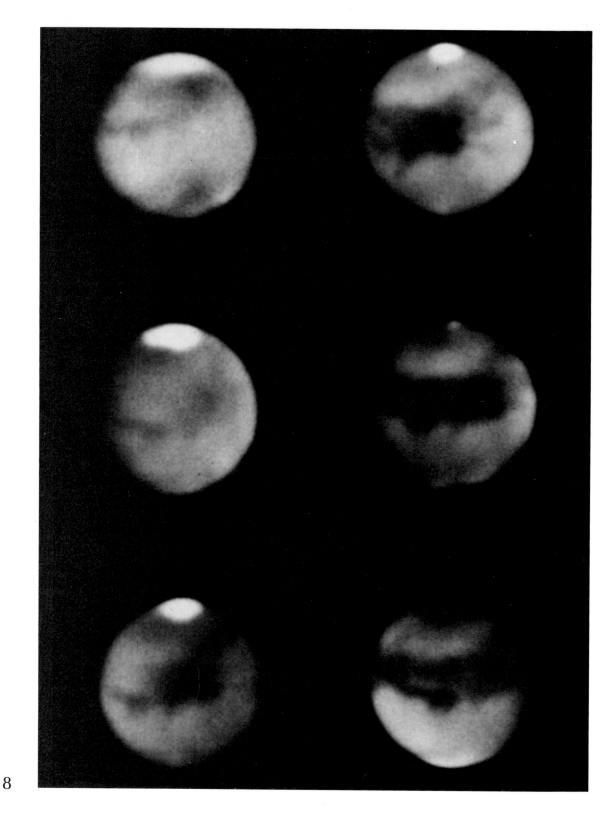

8

Very long ago, when people saw what they called the Red Planet, they were frightened. Since red sometimes makes people think of blood, some people feared that war and killing were coming.

These early people named the red planet Mars. Mars is the Roman god of war. The symbol for the planet Mars is a shield and a sword.

Over the centuries, astronomers have tried to learn more about this unusual planet. In 1784, Sir William Herschel, a German-born astronomer, was looking at Mars through his telescope. He was startled to see large white areas around the north and south poles of the planet. He decided that these were ice caps like those around the poles of planet Earth.

Herschel also noticed that the surface of Mars was not always the same. It seemed to change from light to dark red with the seasons during the Earth year. Herschel wondered if Mars had seasons and weather like Earth. Could there be living beings on Mars, too?

The ice caps at the poles of Mars seen at different times of the year.

About one hundred years later, an Italian astronomer, Giovanni Schiaparelli, noticed about forty thin, dark lines on Mars. He called them *canali*. In Italian, *canali* means "channels". Channels are natural waterways, such as the English Channel.

But *canali* sounds like the English word "canal". So people who spoke English thought the *canali* on Mars were like canals on Earth. Most canals, such as the Panama Canal, are dug by humans. Therefore, some people got the wrong idea. They thought that the "canals" on Mars had been made by living beings.

Giovanni Schiaparelli

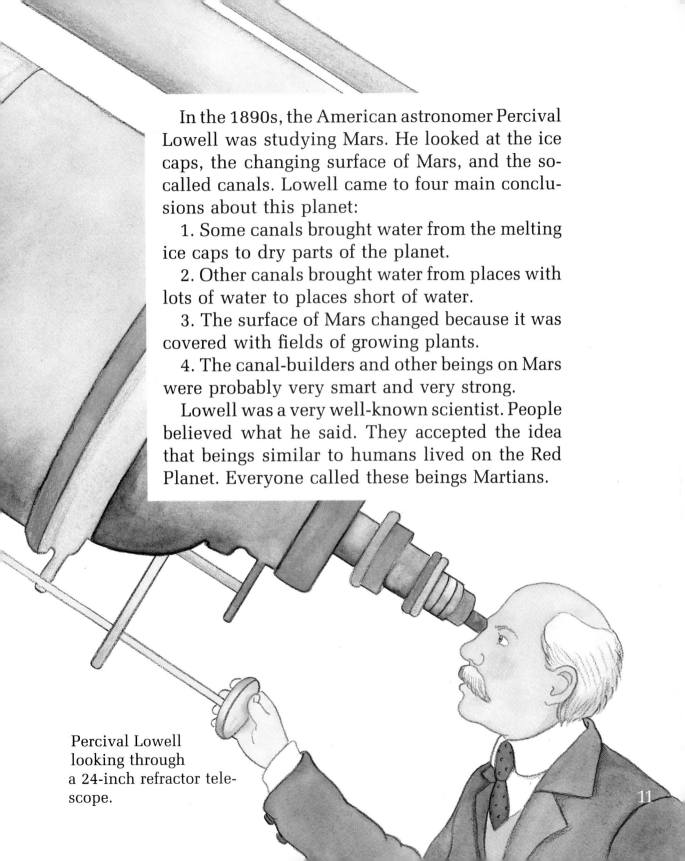

In the 1890s, the American astronomer Percival Lowell was studying Mars. He looked at the ice caps, the changing surface of Mars, and the so-called canals. Lowell came to four main conclusions about this planet:

1. Some canals brought water from the melting ice caps to dry parts of the planet.

2. Other canals brought water from places with lots of water to places short of water.

3. The surface of Mars changed because it was covered with fields of growing plants.

4. The canal-builders and other beings on Mars were probably very smart and very strong.

Lowell was a very well-known scientist. People believed what he said. They accepted the idea that beings similar to humans lived on the Red Planet. Everyone called these beings Martians.

Percival Lowell looking through a 24-inch refractor telescope.

"The Martians Are Coming!"

On Halloween Eve, October 30, 1938, many Americans were listening to a program of dance music on the CBS Radio Network. Suddenly, the broadcast was interrupted.

The announcer read an urgent news bulletin. People had seen brilliant flashes of light coming from Mars.

After the news, the dance music started again. A few minutes later, the announcer cut in once more. He sighed deeply after he reported the latest development. A blazing meteor had just landed in New Jersey!

NEWSROOM

Soon the network had a reporter at the scene. In great excitement he told how Martians were pouring out of their spaceship. They were turning their deadly heat-ray guns on anyone within range.

All at once, the reporter's voice was cut off. It sounded as though he had been killed by a Martian.

Other announcers picked up the story. They described the Martians' conquest of New Jersey. And they warned that the Martians were advancing on New York City.

Panic spread among the listeners. Some grabbed their belongings, jumped in cars, and started driving away from the menace. Others locked the doors and windows of their houses, and hid in basements and cellars.

A few brave souls went out to fight the invaders. In New Jersey, a group of farmers thought they saw the Martian spaceship. They fired their rifles at a strange, dark shape.

By the end of the radio program, everyone realized what had happened. The invasion of the Martians was a made-up story. But more than one million people had believed what they heard. Most of them had taken every word to be true.

The farmers who had fired on the "spaceship" were most embarrassed. The morning following the broadcast, they found that they had shot several holes in the town's water tower!

People were easily fooled because they wanted to believe there were intelligent beings on Mars. Some went even further: They were sure that Martians wanted to conquer Earth.

Exploring Mars from Earth

Radio and television programs, books, and movies invent lots of stories about Mars. But astronomers are also making many exciting, true-to-life discoveries about the Red Planet.

In the year 1877, astronomer Asaph Hall, in Washington, D.C., made an astounding discovery. He found that Mars, like Earth, has a moon. In fact, he saw that Mars has two moons! He gave them Greek names: Phobos ("fear") and Deimos ("panic"). According to Greek legend, Phobos and Deimos were the sons of Mars, the god of war.

Asaph Hall

Phobos looks like a big, black potato in the sky. It tumbles about as it circles Mars. Although Phobos is the larger of the two moons, it is quite small. It is only 17 miles in diameter. Earth's moon is much bigger — over 2,000 miles in diameter.

The path Phobos follows around Mars is called its orbit. The orbit of Phobos is very close to Mars. It is only about 3,750 miles from the surface of Mars. Earth's moon's orbit is 240,000 miles away.

The other Mars moon, Deimos, has the same potato shape as Phobos. But it is much smaller. It is less than 10 miles long. Deimos's orbit is far from the planet, about 12,000 miles.

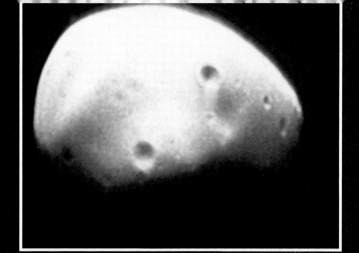

Right: Deimos, Mars's smaller moon, has some large craters.

Below: Phobos, the larger moon, with Mars in the background.

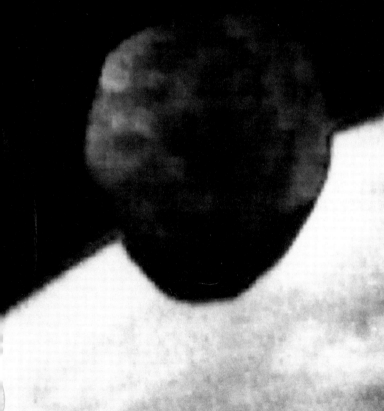

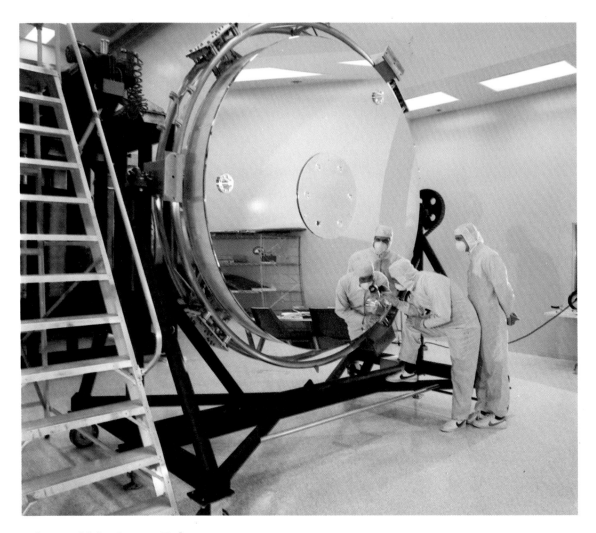

The Hubble Space Telescope.

Modern astronomers have many new tools to help them. With bigger and better telescopes and with spacecrafts they can see many more details on the surface of Mars. Other advanced instruments measure the temperature of Mars. They tell what chemicals are on the surface. They pick out different gasses in the atmosphere.

What have the scientists found?

Mars is very cold and very dry. Scattered across the surface are many giant volcanoes. Lava covers much of the land.

In Mars' northern half, or hemisphere, is a huge raised area. It is about 2,500 miles wide. Astronomers call this the Great Tharsis Bulge.

Left: Four volcanoes in the northern half of Mars are the circular areas. To the far left is Olympus Mons. The row of three volcanoes are Arsia Mons, Pavonis Mons, and Ascraeus Mons.

Below: Olympus Mons.

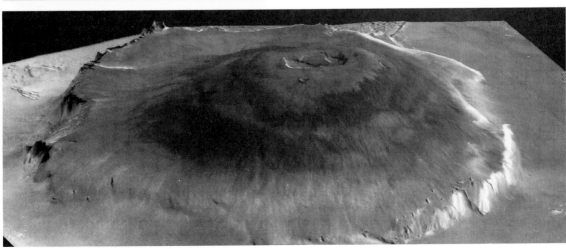

There are four mammoth volcanoes on the Great Tharsis Bulge. The largest one is Mount Olympus, or Olympus Mons. It is the biggest mountain on Mars. Some think it may be the largest mountain in the entire solar system.

Mount Olympus is 15 miles high. At its peak is a 50-mile-wide basin. Its base is 375 miles

An artist made this model of the basin of Mount Olympus using photographs taken by *Mariner 9*.

across. That's nearly as big as the state of Texas!

375 miles wide

Mauna Loa, in Hawaii, is the largest volcano on Earth. Yet, compared to Mount Olympus, Mauna Loa looks like a little hill. The Hawaiian volcano is only 5½ miles high. Its base, on the bottom of the Pacific Ocean, is just 124 miles wide.

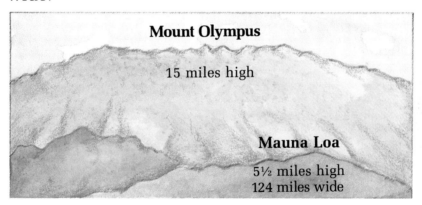

Mount Olympus

15 miles high

Mauna Loa

5½ miles high
124 miles wide

Each of the other three volcanoes in the Great Tharsis Bulge are over 10 miles high. They are named Arsia Mons, Pavonis Mons, and Ascraeus Mons.

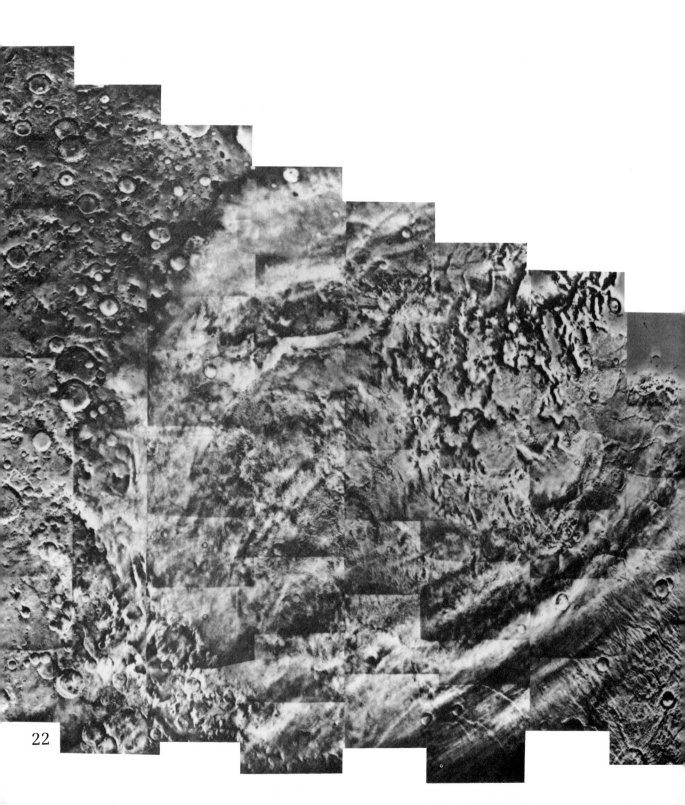

The southern half, or hemisphere, of Mars has no big volcanoes. But it does have lots and lots of craters — giant holes in the ground. The craters have been dug by meteorites. Meteorites are pieces of stone and metal that smash into a planet from outer space.

Some craters on Mars are enormous. The largest one is Hellas Planitia ("Greek Plain"). It is about 1,000 miles wide. (That's the same distance between Chicago and New Orleans.) And it is four miles deep.

A view of the Hellas Planitia area of Mars in a combination of photos taken by *Viking I.*

Chicago

1,000 miles

New Orleans

Part of the Valles Marineris.

3,000 miles

Los Angeles

New York

The most fantastic sight in the southern hemisphere of Mars is Valles Marineris ("Mariner Valley"). The name comes from the spacecraft that took the first photos of this amazing feature. Valles Marineris is a colossal valley cut in the surface of the planet. From end to end, Valles Marineris is nearly 3,000 miles long. On Earth it would stretch from New York to Los Angeles.

From side to side it is up to 800 miles wide. And in some places, it is almost 4 miles deep from top to bottom. Valles Marineris is 10 times longer, 40 times wider, and twice as deep as the Grand Canyon.

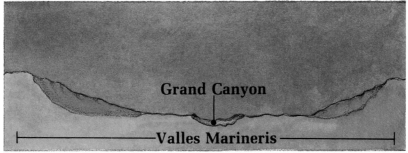

800 miles wide

The grooves near the lower-left section of this photograph taken by *Viking I* show the Valles Marineris.

Some experts say that Valles Marineris was formed by a giant split in the surface of Mars. Since it is near the Great Tharsis Bulge, it may have been caused by the volcanoes. Others think it was dug by a big, powerful river cutting down through the Martian soil.

By the 1960s, scientists had learned much about Mars. Some astronomers then had a wild idea: Let's try to put a human being on the Red Planet.

An artist's painting showing astronauts exploring the Valles Marineris canyons.

Getting Ready to Land

Before scientists dare send a person from Earth to Mars, they must answer some important questions:

- What dangers will face the first astronauts?

- How solid is the surface of Mars?

- What is the climate on Mars?

- Can humans breathe the Mars air?

- Will germs there make them sick?

- Will rays from space kill them?

- Are there Martians?

The only way to get this information would be to put measuring instruments on or near the planet. NASA (National Aeronautics and Space Administration) began a series of flights to Mars and other planets. They called them the *Mariner* series.

Mariner 4 was the first successful flight to Mars. NASA launched *Mariner* 4 in November 1964.

Mariner 4 took nearly eight months to get near the planet. It came as close as 6,000 miles from the surface.

On board *Mariner 4*, a television camera took pictures of the planet. Various instruments measured the temperature, gasses, and radiation around the planet. All the pictures and measurements were sent back to Earth by radio signals.

Early in 1969, scientists blasted *Mariner 6* and *Mariner 7* toward Mars. Their mission was the same as that of *Mariner 4*. But *Mariners 6* and *7* were more advanced spacecrafts. They came within 2,000 miles of Mars, and took much better pictures of the Red Planet.

Mariner 9, sent in 1971, was even more special. It got as close as 860 miles from the surface. It continued to orbit Mars for nearly a year. *Mariner 9* sent back over 7,000 excellent photos taken by its two cameras.

Experts carefully studied the photos taken by all the *Mariners*. They did not see any sign of growing plants. Nor could they find any trace of animals. They decided there is probably no life on Mars.

Furthermore, they discovered that Mars is being bombarded by cosmic rays and ultraviolet rays. These rays are deadly. They would kill most forms of life that we know about.

Canali, the scientists realized, are surely not canals. Perhaps the early astronomers saw long rows of big rocks and boulders. At sunrise or sunset they cast shadows that may have looked like canals from Earth. Or maybe the splotchy, colored surface made them think they saw straight lines.

Canals are definitely missing on Mars. But there are some cracks in the surface. They look like dry riverbeds on Earth.

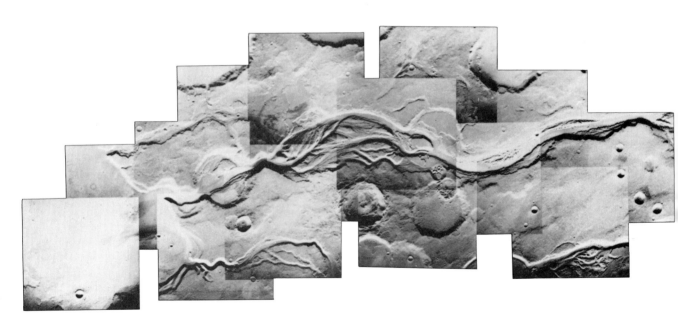

Above: A group of photos taken by *Viking I* shows a winding, braided channel, probably made by water.

Facing Page: A photo taken by *Mariner 9* shows a river bed hundreds of miles long.

Perhaps Mars once had lots of flowing water. At that time, the climate must have been much warmer. Over thousands or millions of years, the climate changed. The temperature dropped extremely low. Water froze in the ground. Some froze in the ice caps. Today, scientists believe that Mars does not have even one drop of water in liquid form!

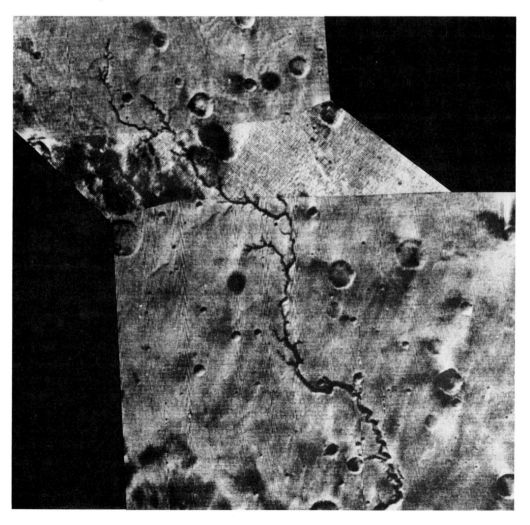

Modern scientists have also found that Herschel was right about the ice caps. Frozen caps surround the north and south poles of Mars. These caps are mostly frozen carbon dioxide. Frozen carbon dioxide is sometimes called dry ice.

The surface of Mars is made up of dusty soil, much like the deserts on Earth. But Martian soil is red. It contains twice as much iron as the soil on Earth. And this iron is rusted, which is why it is reddish-brown in color.

Scientists now know why Herschel saw the color of Mars change from dark to light. It's because of Mars' violent dust storms. The dust storms blow away the top layer of soil, which is light red. Then the layer below is exposed. This lower layer is darker in color.

Dust storms rage on Mars. Powerful winds gust as high as 300 miles per hour. They send up huge towers of swirling dust. Sometimes these towers reach three miles in height. Dust storms can cover the entire planet.

The rocky plain of Mars looks like some desert landscapes on earth.

Getting Set

In July and September of 1976, NASA blasted two spacecraft toward Mars. *Viking I* landed on Mars on July 20, 1976. *Viking II* landed on September third.

Because astronomers wanted to explore two different parts of Mars, they set down the *Viking* spacecraft at two points about 1,800 miles apart.

Each *Viking* space ship was really made up of two separate craft. The main part, like *Mariner 9*, went into orbit around Mars. And from there it took photos of the planet.

The other part of *Viking* looked like a small, crab-shaped automobile. It was called the lander. The lander touched down on the surface of Mars.

A model of the *Viking* lander. The lander, about the size of a compact car, has instruments to measure and test the surface and atmosphere on Mars.

A model of the *Viking* spacecraft.

Immediately its camera went to work. Radio signals flashed pictures back to scientists on Earth. The pictures showed a surface much like the deserts of the American Southwest. Most striking was the sandy, blood-red soil and the immense numbers of rocks strewn about.

The *Mariner* probes had ruled out large living plants or animals on Mars. Now scientists wanted to find out if there are any tiny forms of life on Mars. Such small living beings are called germs or microbes. On Earth, microbes live everywhere — in soil, air, and water.

The *Vikings* were designed to search for microbes. Each one had a robot arm with a small shovel at the end. Scientists sent radio signals to the arm. The arm scooped up samples of Martian soil. Then it dumped the samples into three tiny laboratories inside the lander. Each laboratory tested the soil in a different way and radioed back the results. Experts went over the figures again and again. Finally, they reached a decision. The samples definitely showed no sign of microbes or other forms of life.

But then, in August 1996, everything changed. NASA scientists had been studying twelve meteorites that had come from Mars and landed on Earth. In one meteorite they made an amazing discovery. Fossils of microbes! They might be signs that life existed on Mars some three billion years ago!

When the Mars meteorite was put on display in the Smithsonian's National Museum of Natural History in 1996, it attracted a lot of attention.

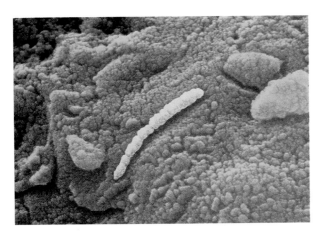

One of the tubelike microbes discovered on the meteorite stands out in this greatly magnified photograph. (The tube is colored yellow to make it easier to see.) Scientists believe these tubes prove there was once life on Mars.

Each fossil was a microscopic speck, golden in color. And each one was a tiny little tube, much thinner than a human hair. Could these be living microbes? Scientists are testing and examining these tubes to learn more. They are still not sure of their findings. But at last there are signs of life on Mars!

The exploration of Mars goes on. NASA launched two unmanned flights to Mars in November 1996. The *Mars Pathfinder* has a roving vehicle, *Sojourner*. It is designed to roll around the surface and sample chemicals in the Martian rocks and soil. The *Mars Global Surveyor* will orbit the planet to map the surface and study the atmosphere. And there are plans for ten more unmanned flights in the next ten years.

Now, more than ever, scientists are hard at work. Some day soon, they hope to land the first humans on Mars.

An idea for an international space station, called Space Station Freedom, is designed to be about 500 feet across and 200 feet high.

Getting There

Getting to Earth's moon is a baby step compared to the giant leap from Earth to Mars. The Earth's moon is 240,000 miles away. But Mars is 50 million miles away. That's over 200 times as far. The trip to Mars will take about eleven months.

The final plans for getting the astronauts to Mars are still far from certain. One plan will place a space station in orbit around Earth. The space station will be big enough for humans to live in for long periods of time.

Shuttles will carry spaceships, food, fuel, equipment, and eight astronauts to the space station. Rockets going to Mars will also blast off from this space station.

An artist's picture of a mission on Mars. Rovers gather scientific data and send it to the orbiter in space, which sends it to Earth.

Using the space station as a jumping-off point will save a tremendous amount of fuel. Earth's gravity is strongest right at the surface. The higher you go, the weaker the pull of gravity and the less fuel that is needed.

When all is ready, the people on the space station will launch a cargo ship without astronauts. The cargo ship will carry fuel and supplies. It will also carry a smaller craft to land on Mars.

The cargo ship will go into orbit around Mars. After it is in place, an eight-person crew will blast off from the space station in another spaceship. The crew will attach their ship to the cargo ship.

Some of the crew members will remain in the cargo craft. They will be ready to help in an emergency. The other astronauts will climb into the landing craft and fly down to the surface of Mars.

These astronauts will explore the Red Planet. Dressed in space suits, they will collect samples, run experiments, make observations, and learn how to survive on Mars.

After about a month, the astronauts on Mars will use the landing craft again. This time it will lift them off the surface of Mars to join up with the cargo ship.

Then they will all rocket back to the space station. From there they can take the short, easy flight home.

The second plan for reaching Mars would not use a space station. It would use a super-powerful rocket to carry the people and supplies all the way to Mars. But this mission would have a crew of only six, not eight, astronauts.

One thing is certain. Many new and better ideas will come along before that exciting day when the first astronauts blast off for Mars.

Walking and Breathing on Mars

Mars is about half the size of Earth. A straight line through Earth from the north pole to the south pole measures nearly 8,000 miles. The same line on Mars is just over 4,000 miles long.

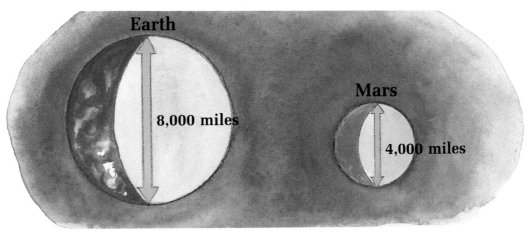

The pull of a planet's gravity is based on its mass. Since Mars has much less mass than Earth, its gravity is much weaker. The pull of gravity on Mars is only a little more than one-third as strong as on Earth.

Suppose the astronauts each weigh about 150 pounds on Earth. With the weaker gravity, they would weigh less than 60 pounds on Mars. They would feel light and bouncy. Every step would be twice as long as on Earth. Astronauts could jump higher, run faster, throw farther, and lift heavier weights. In fact, they could easily break Olympic records set on Earth.

But the weak gravity on Mars also causes major problems for humans. Without the constant pull of a strong gravity, the astronauts' muscles would become weak and flabby. Their bones would become thin and brittle. To keep fit on Mars, the astronauts would have to exercise daily.

60 pounds

Mars

Earth

150 pounds

**8/1,000ths
of a pound**

Mars

The air pressure on Mars is much less than on Earth. On Mars the air pressure is a tiny fraction ($^8/_{1,000ths}$) of a pound per square inch. On Earth, the air pressure is nearly 15 pounds per square inch. Human lungs are filled with air under high pressure. The weak Mars air pressure would cause the air to burst out of people's lungs.

The make-up of Martian air is also quite different. Ninety-five percent is carbon dioxide, with only a tiny bit of oxygen. On Earth, 21 percent of the air is oxygen. To spend even a few minutes on Mars, the astronauts must carry their own supply of oxygen.

Mars is very much colder than Earth. The coldest spot on Mars is at the south pole. The temperature is around 220° below zero Fahrenheit (F). The warmest place is at the Mars Equator. Here, the temperature reaches a high of about 50°F. On Earth, the average temperature ranges from 72° below zero F at the south pole to 94°F along the equator.

15 pounds

Earth

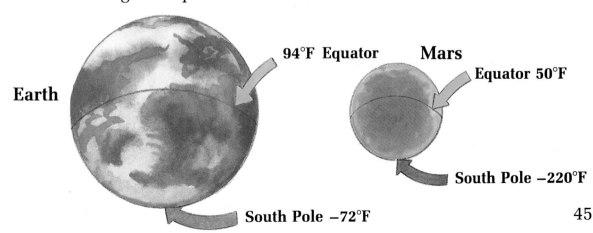

Earth

94°F Equator

Mars

Equator 50°F

South Pole −220°F

South Pole −72°F

Time Out for Mars

A year is the time it takes for a planet to make one trip around the sun. The length of the year depends on two things — the distance the planet must cover in one orbit, and the speed of the moving planet.

Planets farther away from the sun have longer orbits than closer planets. Earth's orbit is 584 million miles long. But Mars' orbit is 890 million miles.

Earth also moves faster than Mars. Earth travels around the sun at a speed of 66,500 miles per hour. Mars goes only 54,000 miles per hour in its orbit.

Jupiter

Mars

Earth

Sun

Mercury

Venus

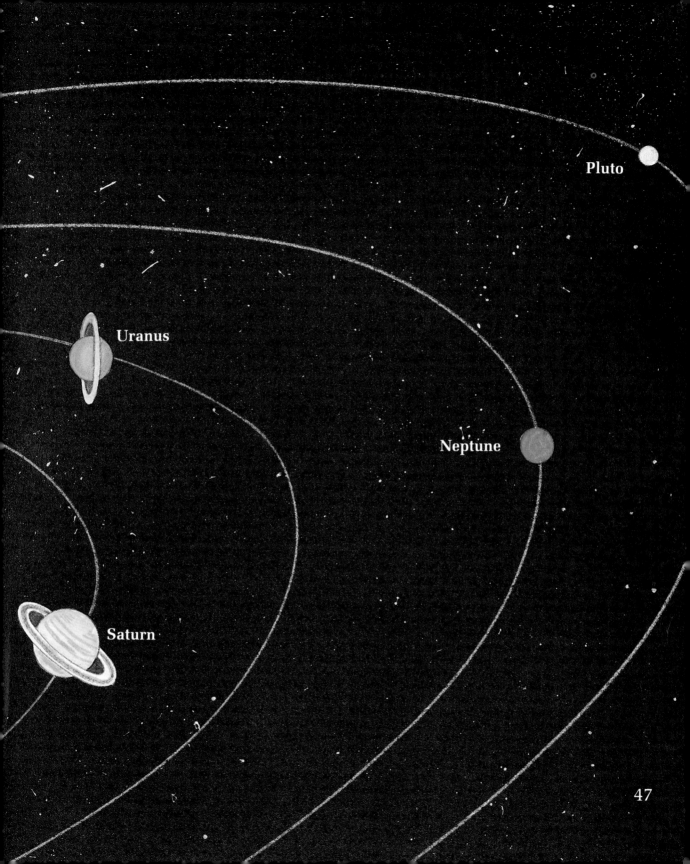

Pluto

Uranus

Neptune

Saturn

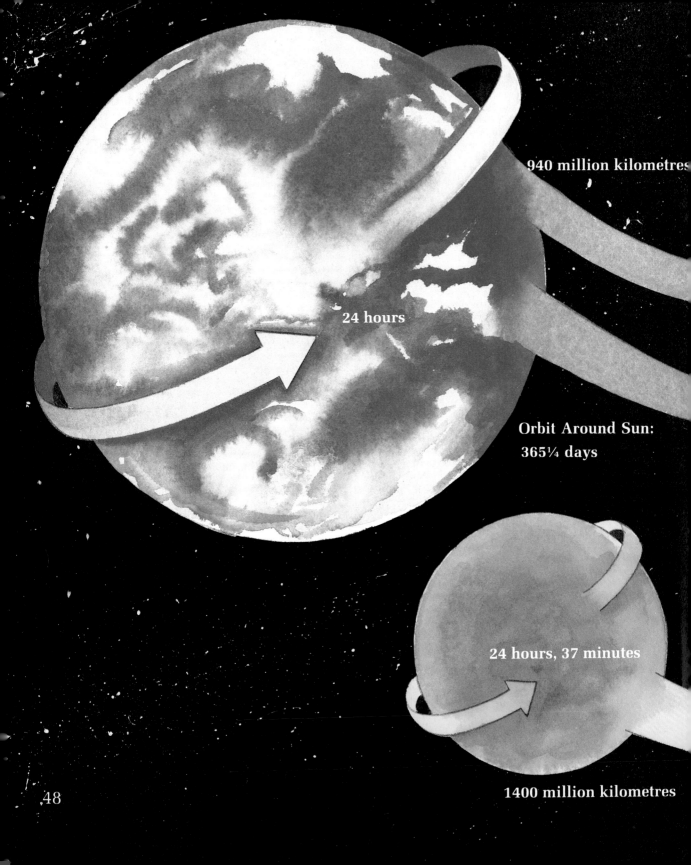

940 million kilometres

24 hours

Orbit Around Sun:
365¼ days

24 hours, 37 minutes

1400 million kilometres

48

As you know, it takes Earth just over 365 days to make a complete orbit. Because of the longer journey and slower speed, Mars only gets around once every 687 days. So, a year on Mars is 687 days long.

On Mars, a year is nearly twice as long as a year on Earth. But a Martian day is only a little longer than an Earth day.

All planets spin, or rotate, as they orbit the sun. A day is the time it takes for one complete rotation. It takes Earth twenty-four hours to make one complete rotation.

Mars spins more slowly than Earth. The slower speed makes a Mars day longer than an Earth day. It takes Mars twenty-four hours and thirty-seven minutes to turn around completely.

A view of sunset on Mars taken by *Viking I.*

Orbit Around Sun: 687 days

Making Mars More Like Earth

Terraforming was originally a word from science fiction. It means changing a planet to make it more like Earth.

At first, all the ideas for terraforming Mars came from science fiction. One wild scheme was to start a nuclear reaction in Phobos or Deimos. The reaction would make the moon of Mars into a tiny sun. Its heat would pour down on the frozen planet. The heat would melt the water frozen in the permafrost. The result would be flowing streams and ponds of fresh water.

Another fanciful notion was to capture some of the ice that forms the rings of the planet Saturn. A powerful space ship would then tow the ice to Mars. As the ice melted, it would provide water for the planet.

Still other writers considered exploding atom bombs in the volcanoes on Mars. This would send out hot gases that would create an atmosphere. The heat would warm the entire planet, melting all the frozen water.

An artist's picture of astronauts laying out materials to capture the sun's rays.

Most recently, some serious scientists started thinking about terraforming Mars. One idea is to use immense mirrors to reflect and focus the sun's rays onto the surface of Mars. This would raise the temperature of the planet and melt the frozen water.

The mirrors they have in mind are not the usual glass mirrors. Rather, they are thin, light, shiny plastic panels. The plastic is much lighter than glass. They can be made into mirrors as big as a half-mile square!

Suppose scientists succeed in placing eight gigantic mirrors in orbit around Mars. The heat the mirrors reflect would melt the permafrost. That would produce liquid water. It also would release water vapor. This gas would enter the air around Mars. It would help give it an atmosphere more like Earth's.

At the same time, the experts suggest using special plants to make Mars more livable. These plants are called blue-green algae. They are tiny plants without roots, stems, or leaves. Blue-green algae are the only kinds of plants that grow around Earth's south pole. You know that Mars has a climate somewhat like our south pole. Perhaps the blue-green algae will also grow on Mars.

Blue-green algae, like other plants, take in carbon dioxide and release oxygen. Mars' air, we said, has a lot of carbon dioxide and almost no oxygen. So, lots of algae growing on Mars might change the balance. It might even produce enough oxygen to sustain human life.

Finally, the scientists are thinking of using gasses known as CFCs (chlorofluorocarbons). On Earth, air conditioners and refrigerators use CFCs. Some of these gasses leak into the atmosphere. They then destroy the ozone high above Earth and expose humans to dangerous rays from outer space.

But Mars does not have any ozone. So the CFCs would not do any harm there. The CFCs would allow the heat from the sun's light to warm the surface of Mars. Yet they would not let the warmth escape back into space. The heat would build up and raise the temperature of Mars. Mars would become more like Earth. Scientists believe it might take perhaps 100,000 years of change to make Mars more like Earth.

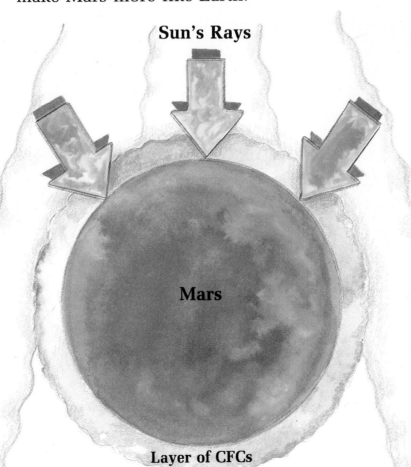

Sun's Rays

Mars

Layer of CFCs

A Mars like Earth would be very different from the planet we know today. It might be more the way scientists think it was long ago. The planet would have lots of liquid water in rivers, lakes, and oceans. The atmosphere would be warm enough to allow living things to grow.

The push to learn more about Mars continues. During the next century the first astronauts will probably land on our neighbor in space. After that, others surely will follow. Mars could be a livable place for plants in perhaps 100 to 10,000 years. And perhaps it will have an atmosphere livable for humans, even if it will be 100,000 years from now.

The future is very exciting indeed!

This image of Mars was taken by the Hubble Space Telescope. Bluish clouds cover the icy north pole.

An artist's picture of astronauts exploring Phobos, with Mars in the background.

Cover photo credits:

Front cover:

Taken by the *Viking* orbiter, this "fish-eye" view of Mars shows the gigantic Valles Marineris canyon system (running across center) and the heavily cratered southern hemisphere.

Back cover, clockwise from top right:

Close-up view of the caldera of Olympus Mons. The walls of this volcano tower fifteen miles above the plain.

Computer-generated, false-color exaggeration of the color variations on Mars. Atmospheric haze, frost, and deserts are turquoise, white, and yellow. Dark materials are red and blue. The volcanoes are dark red.

Artist's model of a cargo vehicle for a mission to Mars.

Many photos taken by *Viking I* are put together to show the Mangala Callis. These channels seem to have been carved by running water.

Interior photo and illustration credits:

Photos:

California Institute of Technology and Carnegie Institute of Washington:
page 7.

Hughes Aircraft Company:
page 18.

NASA:
pages 8, 16-17, 19 (top), 20, 22-23, 24, 25, 26-27, 30, 31, 32, 34, 35, 36-37, 39, 40, 41, 49, 51, 55, 56, back cover.

USGS Flagstaff:
page 19 (bottom).

USGS/Science Photo Library:
front cover.

AP/Wide World Photos:
page 38.

Illustrations © 1992 by Joan Holub:

pages 10, 11, 12-13, 14-5, 21, 25, 43, 44, 45, 46-47, 48-49, 53.